Praise for Life List

"Exquisite in its celebration of flight and how wilderness works its way into our blood and bones and calls us to something transcendent." —Shann Ray, author of *American Masculine* and *Atomic Theory 7*

"Like a rapt man with one eye pressed to a microscope, it is Beaudin's job to look—to look carefully. He reports back with equal care, and the paths he takes us down are delightful." —Michael Earl Craig, former Montana poet laureate

"Beaudin's poems dip and swerve and caw; if you listen closely enough, you might just begin to understand that the ache of the human heart can only be translated through the language of crows." —Meg Kearney, author of *An Unkindness of Ravens*

"A deftly woven catalogue of human experience through the keen observations of birds and landscapes. Beaudin masterfully translates the mysterious language between magpies and mountains and weaves it into a beautifully poetic tapestry." —Michael Garrigan, author of *Robbing the Pillars*

"Beaudin's poems ask us to pay attention not only to birds, but to our dreams, to the music that circles around us all." —Taylor Brorby, author of *Crude: Poems*

"Beaudin's poems ground us long enough to take flight in this outdoor field guide of an interior life." —Mark Gibbons, author of *The Imitation Blues* and *Mostly Cloudy*

"It has always been the poet's job to name what's at stake in this moment, but now, it is their sacred calling. Beaudin delivers beautifully." —Winona Bateman, poet and climate organizer with Families for a Livable Climate

Other titles from Riverfeet Press

THIS SIDE OF A WILDERNESS: A Novel (2013)
- Daniel J. Rice

THE UNPEOPLED SEASON: Journal from a North Country
Wilderness (2014) - Daniel J. Rice

WITHIN THESE WOODS: A collection of Northwoods nature
essays with original illustrations by the author (2015)
- Timothy Goodwin

ECOLOGICAL IDENTITY: Finding Your Place in a Biological
World (2016) - Timothy Goodwin

TEACHERS IN THE FOREST: Essays from the last wilderness in
Mississippi Headwaters country (2016) - Barry Babcock

ROAD TO PONEMAH: The Teachings of Larry Stillday (2016)
- Michael Meuers

A FIELD GUIDE TO LOSING YOUR FRIENDS (2017)
- Tyler Dunning

AWAKE IN THE WORLD (2017): a collection of stories, poems,
and essays about wildlife, adventure, and the environment

ONE-SENTENCE JOURNAL (winner of the 2018 Montana Book
Award and the 2019 High Plains Book Award) - Chris La Tray

WILDLAND WILDFIRES: and where the wildlife go (2018)
- Randie Adams

I SEE MANY THINGS: Ninisidawenemaag, Book I (2019)
- Erika Bailey-Johnson

AWAKE IN THE WORLD, V.II (2019): a collection of stories, po-
ems, and essays about wildlife, adventure, and the environment

FAMILIAR WATERS (2020) - David Stuver

BURNT TREE FORK: A Novel (2020) - J.C. Bonnell

REGARDING WILLINGNESS (2020) - Tom Harpole

LIFE LIST

LIFE LIST

poems

Marc Beaudin

For Dee
A muse for the ages
Still my favorite
Bartender (now,
after Ma).
Love Brad
"Freudhie"

Riverfeet Press

Riverfeet Press
Livingston, MT 59047
www.riverfeetpress.com

First Edition

LIFE LIST

Poetry

Marc Beaudin

Copyright 2020 © by the author

Monotypes copyright 2020 © by Storrs Bishop

All rights reserved.

ISBN-13: 978-1-7324968-7-3

LCCN: 2020949462

This title is available at a special discount to booksellers and libraries. Send inquiries to: riverfeetpress@gmail.com.

Cover design by Megan Eubank

Mayfly illustration by Timothy Goodwin

Typesetting & interior design by Daniel J. Rice

Riverfeet Press is proud to be Made in Montana.

for William Heyen

Northern Cardinal

CONTENTS

Introduction

Splitting Hairs Counting Feathered Things

Ornithology is a discipline born of wishful obsession. From our ancestors who watched birds leave gravity's binding tethers somewhere on the plains of Africa, the fascination with feathers and flight have been ever present in our being. Watchfulness is both art and science whether practiced by multiple-degreed professionals, globe-trotting rarity seekers or backyard feeders. In the noticing, most watchers can't help but record what they see. By day and date. By season and place – state, city or local patch – most attend to some kind of list. They note what's what, what's where and when it's there. Many record on paper, but most likely have the records scribed now bit by bit in some digital format. Bird by bird the variety accrues. Year by year the life list grows. By what we know, or think we know, there are almost 10,000 species in the Class Aves to see. Some have come close to that, but no one has ever seen every one.

The listing compulsion is dyed deeply into the fabric of who we are. Perhaps it began with someone wanting to know which bird could fly fast and which one would run first before taking off. The runner more likely to be slain for the next meal, and the fast flier becoming a being worthy of admiration for wariness and swift flight. Over time, the names came. By color, mode of behavior or song sung. No bird was ignored by status. Every bird regardless of its point of origin mattered. We had yet to become too smart to understand that despite the Latin labels Linnaeus laid on living things, they already knew who they were.

But ego prevails, and we are yet possessed with the

pigeon-holing game. We split. Lump. Split again. The DNA hairs have become razor thin, then halved repeatedly. This bird formerly that bird is the same bird it always was. It gets added then subtracted then divided into races. Some worry over what they lose, list-wise. Others celebrate the gain.

Committees gather and debate. Birds with labels that offend get identities remade. The listing goes on. From primal noticing back then to e-birding now, little has changed. In the end, when time is done and we're in the ground or dust in the wind, no one else will remember or care how many birds we've counted. What will matter is if any will be left for those listers yet to come.

In *Life List*, Marc Beaudin turns away from the taxonomic to the humanly tactile topics of social justice (injustice), environmental degradation, and identifies beyond field marks to feeling marked. It is a treatment of birds beyond the ornithological ticking to an obsession with his own introspection. If Emily Dickinson's hope has feathers, then Beaudin's birds have feelings.

Life List is about much more than watching birds. It's about seeing ourselves through them. And if we're lucky, about seeing a bit of them in us. Count yourself fortunate in the reading.

—J. Drew Lanham
author of: *The Home Place: Memoirs of a Colored Man's Love Affair with Nature* and *Sparrow Envy: Poems*

Author's Note

What is the soul if not the sum of the flights of a thousand birds?

It's poor form to quote oneself, but these words from an old poem of mine[1] get to the heart of it. With every passing day, every poem, every bird, I am more convinced of their truth. For many years, crows, herons and other avian species have flown through my poetry, adding their voices and flashes of light to my vain attempts to render in language the precarious circumstances of being alive.

Perhaps my earliest bird-memory is of a summer at dusk, playing in the sand pile out by my grandparents' garden and hearing the low call of a Mourning Dove wafting like a fog from the dark enchantment of the woods we kids called "Snaky Path." The sound scared me, but not enough to run inside where my grandpa would be at his table playing solitaire and my grandma, at her quilting frame or in her rocking chair with knitting needles blazing, peering close against the fading light. The sound was scary, but more so, it held my first Mystery, my first hint that there was some Power in the woods, in the night, in the music-tinged air, that was calling. Something out there that knew my name.

I finished writing this book in a Forest Service cabin at the edge of Montana's Absaroka-Beartooth Wilderness. Those days and nights free of the shackles of electricity, cell service and all the distractive technologies and demands that come with them, gave me the gift of

---

[1] "El Sonido del Mar es Silencio" from *Vagabond Song: Neo-Haibun from the Peregrine Journals*, (Elk River Books, 2015). An earlier version published in *The Moon Cracks Open* (Heal the Earth Press, 2008).

remembering. I remembered who I was, what was important, why I commit myself to this ridiculous passion of putting words on paper — of swinging the hammers of my old typewriter against the brick wall of the page. In these days of climate crisis, the only valid reason to do anything, including our art, is to save the world.

These poems, of course, won't do that. Sometimes I doubt anything will. But we must never stop trying. The assurance of failure should never prevent the attempt. It's too important, and we just might be wrong.

What is the soul if not the sum of the flights of a thousand birds?

This line, gifted to me over 20 years ago by whatever Mystery it is that holds our poetry, states more clearly, more fully, my relationship to the Feathered Ones than anything else I could attempt to articulate. Every poem in this collection is, at essence, merely a slower way of speaking those same words.

— Marc Beaudin
September 17, 2020
Glenn's Bar, Livingston, MT

LIFE LIST

Birds of the Eastern United States

"… when I breathe with the birds,
The spirit of wrath becomes the spirit of blessing,
And the dead begin from their dark to sing in my sleep."

— Theodore Roethke, "Journey to the Interior"

Canada Goose

The Things We've Lost *(Branta canadensis)*

Wings condense & release
the wintering air as
a ragged vee of geese
pass voiceless overhead

carrying away the things we've lost
like the words, even the sound
of your voice & the three lines
written at your funeral

a clumsy haiku
about your Wild Geese poem
& the rain as usual
This life more & more

seems just a series of things
lost. A leaking bucket carried
from a well up a long trail
till finally we're home

with only a few drops
to sustain us
but somehow
that's enough

Carbon *(Pelecanus occidentalis)*

Driving late night through the pass
with narcoleptic mountains pressing in
from either side & Coltrane struggling
through the static of the radio while

whitebark pines are dead & dying right
outside my window & pelicans & sea
turtles are dead & dying, still, in
the black waters of the Gulf & Éliane

Parenteau, age 93, Alyssa Charest Bégnoche,
age 4, & 45 others dead along the
tracks in Lac-Mégantic but then the radio
clears & a horn sounds out pure as fire

For a moment any future is possible

Until I realize the passenger door is
ajar & the noise & smell of the wind
writhing through the breech become a
presence seated next to me & when, by

degrees this presence becomes palpable
enough to see from the corner of my
eye I speed up & say,
"I knew you'd have dark hair."

Common Loon

Loon Point *(Gavia immer)*

Red stone eye holds the setting sun
final embers of wildfire &
all the blood raging in my veins. The loon

erupts beside my canoe fixing me
forever in that moment with his terrible
transcendent eye. And his voice:

the laughter of one driven mad
by the incessant pounding at the door of the world
Who's there? in the other devil's name. His

silhouette in flight mimicked by this
peninsula cutting halfway across the lake
giving it a new name known only to me

until now. You too now know the secret
but must promise to keep it to yourself
to use only if you someday come here

Great Blue Heron

Another Blue *(Ardea herodias)*

Voice of the heron carries the
rasp of pterodactyl & archaeopteryx
Is an unmarked grave that reaches

suddenly with taloned fingers &
startles the man swimming alone
among cattails and mud-sleeping turtles

He once, years before, carried a dead heron close
to his chest like an infant – this old
friend & father, teacher in the school of

lake water & moonlight, omen,
bringer of dreams, found in the reeds
at lake's edge, waiting

From his canoe, aluminum turned brass in
evening light, he watches the bird's spirit, or
something, fly from the willows, bank above

the still water & disappear over the mosaic
of trees climbing the hillside. Today
standing thigh-deep in the marsh

he rubs that memory between thumb
& finger, enjoys the sun sinking into face
& shoulders & tries to ignore

the insistent buzzing of an airplane
like some small insect, trapped
at the kitchen window

Mortality *(Phalacrocorax auritus)*

Scarecrow Island recedes
as cormorants follow our wake
cutting leaden waters &
churning up a feast of fish

Perhaps not a moment passes
in this world of piercing beauty
without some little death
Today the fish, tomorrow you & I

The horizon swallows the island
& someday my favorite fedora
will sell for a few dollars
at a downtown thrift store

Murder of the Stag *(Charadrius vociferus)*

Killdeer in a vacant lot
of gravel & concrete-sundering weeds
fakes a broken wing
to lead the predator in me
away from her nest

The prey in me can sympathize
being full like a post-holiday
garbage truck
with its own vain attempts
to protect what I love

Roethke's German translator
unfamiliar with any such bird
rendered the word as "murder of the stag"
& we laughed about it around our jug
of cheap wine surrounded by the ghosts of roses

I touched the ground, the ground warmed
by the murder of the stag
the salt laughed, and the stones
It works, I suppose
though perhaps a little over the top

Sometimes my broken wing act
is just the thing
to get me through another day

Anhinga

In Excelsis Deo (Anhinga anhinga)

The serpent bird perches
on a dead branch rising from the murk
wings held open to the sun

A terrible god of its world
of one small pond teeming
with supplicant fish that wait

to be released
into the glory of their savior's
stabbing grace

sanctified, spine-shattered,
devoured in the maw
of redemption

The ophidian neck falls back
the red eye reflected on
the face of the water

while a priest of fins & scales
drifts before his flock
demanding songs of praise

My Bones *(Haliaeetus leucocephalus)*

In the blue blue sky of dream
eagle rises
pausing in thunderbird motif
that could resemble, but doesn't,
a crucifixion. Then:

rolls – dives – rises
& pauses again
a page in a book
that always falls open
to this precise spot

Again & again this dance
& it's long after waking
I remember having had
this dream
though all through the morning

I could feel its flight
in my bones

Bald Eagle

Distances *(Zenaida macroura)*

The thing about Mourning Doves
is they always
sound
        far
                away

even when they are
right there
inside
        your
                head

Dreams, Odd *(Larus delawarensis)*

A lone gull takes possession of the river
spiraling down from the dead tree of a utility pole
as you, voiceless in your hospital bed,
draw letters with a finger across your thigh

"D – R – E – A – M – S – O – D – D"
I speak each one as you scratch them out
slowly understanding while a machine
blips out the remaining measure of your life

From the window I can see the gull
a splash of white paint on the brown face
of the river like a woman who's been painting
her bedroom after patching a heart-sized hole

"You've been having odd dreams," I say
trying to fill the silence with sense
Failing. And the river somehow keeps flowing
I guess that's just what rivers do

Tawas Point, Earlier *(Larus smithsonianus)*

A snowdrift of gulls
clusters the narrow strand
a sandbar arcing through the turquoise

We watch pebbles fade
as they dry in our hands
dip them in the waves & watch again

She pins a feather in the sand
One bird draws near
turns & takes the wind

Gathering sand & water
in a salsa jar – she always found
magic in the mundane:

The flight of these gulls
The time we thought would last
The hue & scent of that day

now held in a jar bending
light at my windowsill
back home in a half-empty room

Religion *(Chordeiles minor)*

Nighthawk throws
its single note song
across the darkening sky

Bell of a nearby church
begins to measure out
the remaining hours of the day

These opposites are noted
by a slightly aging man on
his back porch

The pure voice of that darting
wide-mouthed bird catching
insects on the wing

& the frail clanging
of two thousand years' worth
of dogma and delirium

The man considers going inside
Decides to stay as the bell fades
& the bird returns

Messenger *(Bubo virginianus)*

The wave-polished stone fits
the palm of my hand like

a corpse fits the grave like
an infant fits the womb like

my feet fit my footprints
walking the gathering dusk
of this island

The silence swoops inches
from my head pulls

at my soul as the moon
does the ocean. The Great Horned

Owl lands in a tamarack stares
through me. A messenger of death
I've been told

but I know there are many
deaths & most of them bloom

like the moonflower like
small doors swinging open. Then

morning & the sun fills the cave where
I've slept. I open my hand to find the owl's image
embedded in the stone

I slip it into my pocket &
begin the hike, drumbeats rising

from the humus with each step, down
to the dock where a

boat will transport me back
to the world where such things as this
simply do not happen

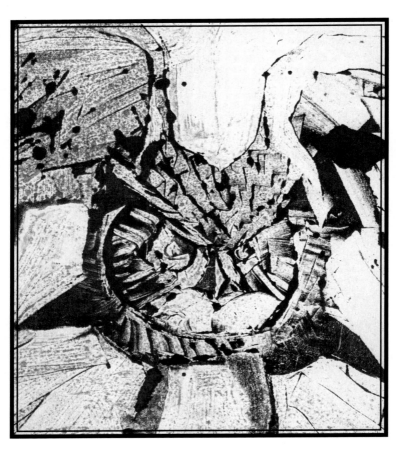

Great Horned Owl

Moonflower *(Megascops asio)*

The moonflower
opens its wings
ghost of a butterfly

Night bleeds from its heart
seeps into the fabric of evening light
& conjures the trill of the owl

from the grove of trees
haunted by memories of ax
& other blades of commerce

The work of pragmatic worms
decaying bits of poetry
congregate to sing through its arms

giving it the courage & thirst
to climb the red trellis
each word it drinks becomes a star

placed one at a time
into the darkening bell of sky
waiting to ring

No Bird: Memory in Translation *(Cyanocitta Cristata)*

A failed poem of a childhood memory
at my grandparents' house
a Blue Jay, an apple crate, summer & all

translated into Turkish
by one of Yusuf's students then, curious,
I use Google to translate it back:

What you left behind that house
If those apple trees are still there
My head was a feather

Under our salt, we expected
I got a little bit of it, I got a little bit of it
Our hearts bumped up like full grains

Maybe it's because we're all deceiving
The hours of those waiting for whispers
I still do not understand anything

A blue jumble
The one who turned me into the world
When the blue blue blinks

Trust me, this version is much better
than the overwritten original
It gets closer to memory's sleight-of-hand

& closer to that bird whose feathers
have no blue pigment, whose color
is nothing but a trick of the light

Linguistics *(Corvus brachyrhynchos)*

The winter crows
are gathering their murder
like holes punched in the sky
They trick the sun
as coyote watches
tries to learn the magic
but always is distracted
by his own dancing shadow

Their movements are silent negotiations
their words hold every dream of flight
on the tip of my tongue
They sharpen
the November-dulled edge
of the treeline
& I check my cheek for blood

Boots crunch snow
heading toward the river
Alone, hungry & all I want
is to understand the language of the crows
Then I will count myself
among the few: the happy ghosts

who sing themselves
to their own
untroubled
sleep

Raven Wind *(Corvus corax)*

Frosted earth splinters fresh-risen sunlight &
bootsteps hush themselves into dead leaves
as ravens discuss the politics of sky & treetop

Walking the slow-breathing trail with
this gift of being awake before the others
I imagine telling you about this moment

when a lone raven passes low overhead
wings cutting the air with the sound
of a soul breaking, finally, free of its body

"Raven wind" I say to no one, knowing
there's no way to quite explain this
to you or any other body-bound soul

What to Pray For *(Passer domesticus)*

The moon cracks open
sparrows fall from its heart:
The world fills with song

But

one perfect bird will die tonight
under the wheels of someone
tuning their radio

Pray that it isn't you

Mortimer *(Sturnus vulgaris)*

> *I'll have a starling shall be taught to speak*
> *Nothing but "Mortimer," and give it him*
> *To keep his anger still in motion.*
> *– Henry IV, Part 1*

Eugene Schiefflin
released 60 starlings in Central Park
1890, the same year
as the massacre at Wounded Knee

He was what they called
a "naturalist" in those days
& thought the park should contain
every bird found in Shakespeare

300 unarmed humans
mostly women & children, half-frozen
became poems before the big guns
of the 7th Cavalry

There are now 200 million starlings
coast to coast, Alaska to Mexico
driving native species from
nesting sites toward extinction

I can't blame the birds
they never chose to enlist
they never asked to be actors
in yet another tragic history

& I can't help loving,
despite the damage they've wrought,
their strange mechanical music
of clicks & whirrs & buzzings

& is their name
from the white gemstone spots
in the night sky
of their winter plumage?

Or from how they resemble
little stars in flight
inspiring Lakota quilts
to cover the bodies of the dead?

Spider Web *(Hylocichla mustelina)*

Each day all that long summer
I was careful with the spider web
barring the doorway of my tent

folding it back gently like opening
a rare book that threatens a cracked
spine under too-rough touch

so the spider had only two
or three strands to reconnect
each day after I left

Some mornings, when the web
resonated with the diamond light of dew
as if holding the song of the Wood Thrush

beginning & ending each day
here – a burst of flutes falling
to an insect's rrzzzz,

I would scuttle out on hands
& knees, ducking my too-full head
to keep the web intact

Such was the rawness of my soul in those days

But when you came out here
with an anger found only in love,
slashed it away in rage meant for me

it clung to your hands like
a nightmare that lingers into morning coffee
& I said nothing

The spider never rebuilt
The dew-painted strings singing sunlight
never returned. How easy it is

to destroy the tenuous beauty
that tries and tries
to fill the wells of our lives

Northern Flicker, Highway 2 *(Colaptes auratus)*

You hold sunlight in your wings
& tail
Fill the pines with a manic laughter

My first sighting, just a flash
of candied gold
& daylight flowed from the darkness of the wood

Now, given the chance to study you
more closely
here is my report for posterity:

Your feathers carry waves of tropical music
Your feet write incomprehensible haiku in the mud
Your eye is the black of the raven at midnight
Your beak is a blade of obsidian
Your tongue is a thorn in search of a crown
Your blood –

is so alarmingly red
& I really am sorry
I was too damn slow hitting the brakes

Northern Flicker

I Declare It Spring *(Agelaius phoeniceus)*

I declare it spring & the calendar be damned
for the Red-winged Blackbird is flashing his epaulets while

the female alights on last year's cattail sending
flurries of cotton down to the marsh the robin

hunts his worm throws music into the trees like
fistfuls of coins I open my coat drinking sunlight

follow a rabbit track into the willows &
dogwood & even the devoured worm sings his song

The Illness of Windows *(Junco hyemalis)*

I fear those shadows most
That start from my own feet.
— Theodore Roethke

Sparrowlike & soft as slate
the Dark-eyed Junco folds into
my hands, neck-broken & free

His body still warm. Even hot.
From the sun? Or the final swelling
of a frantic life as bones found glass?

Or is it my own hands that burn?
I wonder: As he flew into his own reflection
not knowing our illness of windows did he

die believing himself his own rival?
It's absurd to put the obese bulk of human reasoning
into such a small frame but all the same

I have spent years holding windows &
mirrors responsible for the sins of their reflections
never quite looking at what I should

I place the body in the grass deciding against burial
The carrion beetles, perhaps,
have a fondness of glass

Grandma Martyn *(Cardinalis cardinalis)*

This poem is a puzzle
most of the pieces are missing
but it's something about
the last time we walked
together around your yard

The row of apple trees
the line of irises
the remnants of the garden
a million memories of summers
that haunt like welcome scars

& then you took hold
of a branch of that old spruce
the way a mother places
her hand on a child's forehead
checking for fever

High up, unseen,
a cardinal began to sing
the bird marked, I discover later,
with a coupon for Heinz chili sauce
in your worn *Golden Guide* – 10 cents off

Time dripped away from beauty
as unremarkably as always
like icicles beyond the kitchen window
& all those trees replanted
with the houses of a new subdivision

It's good you never saw
their cutting & I hope too
that cardinal was allowed to die
cradled in those branches
long before the saws arrived

Birds of the Western United States

"I pray to the birds because they remind me of what I love rather than what I fear. And at the end of my prayers, they teach me how to listen."

—Terry Tempest Williams, *Refuge*

Snow Geese

Progress *(Chen caerulescens)*

Beyond the desperation diners of Butte
headframes dressed in black
ring of pallbearers around the casket
of the Berkeley Pit – waters 900 feet deep
acidic enough to dissolve a boat

Ten thousand Snow Geese, storm-driven
swirling down from the gun-metal sky

Before the pit, miners descended a mile deep
to blast & scrape the womb of the earth
June 1917, at full production thanks to the gift of war,
the fire takes two days to suffocate 168 miners
time enough to leave notes for those above:

> *If anything happens to me you better sell the house and go*
> *   to California.*
> *We'll meet again, tell mother and the boys goodbye.*

Storm-driven, ten thousand Snow Geese
swirl onto the red water turning it white

> *There's a young fellow here Clarence Marthy,*
> *he has a wife and two kiddies, tell her*
> *we done the best we could but the cards were against us.*

The water recovers from the feathered respite
as thousands upon thousands of geese burn & die

All alive but air getting bad, one small piece
of candle left, think it is all off.

The open pit prevented such old-fashioned disasters
Progress that can be seen from space, the water level
rising ever closer to the groundwater of 30,000 people
& yesterday, a vee of Snow Geese drawn with a shaky hand
pass over my backyard heading roughly toward Butte

[Note: Italicized lines were written by shift boss James Moore who saved
six lives including that of Clarence Marthey (the correct spelling) but lost
his own.]

Mythology Timeline *(Cygnus buccinator)*

Looking west across the Yellowstone
it's impossible to draw the line between
stars & porch lights
but east to the Absarokas untouched
by the frailty of outdoor lighting the stars

are too numerous to see as stars
Cygnus doesn't fly here across a dark sky
rather he swims
through the luminous river of the Milky Way
& I drink in the night like a merlot forgetting

the cheap can of beer in my moon-painted hand
I listen to the longing conversations of
crickets & coyotes
trying to make out the sound of someone's name
but I'm not sure whose, wondering

if that swan is racing toward his love
or away from her

Suce Creek Symphony *(Bonasa umbellus)*

Dancing over stones with
seven sounds resounding over
the bleached bone of a fallen sapling

Arpeggio of water, unbridled
laughter, flash of grouse-fire
drum-thunder from the brush

To read the calligraphy of
moss laced across the wet rock
beneath my boots is a beginning

A beginning, also
when these waters wash
all thought away cacophonating

through the valley past
bowing spruces, bear tracks in the
perfumed mud, the lowing of evening

cows, past the red barn where our goats
settle into corners of straw,
the curve in the road where a rabbit

lies in the tall grass a dead eye to
the sinking sun, past a thousand
small yellow memories that fall

like cottonwood leaves
paper-thin & fading, down
to the hush of the Yellowstone

Glacier Park Toponymy *(Mergus merganser)*

Ghost moon haunts a midday sky
as we hike through firework explosions
of beargrass in riotous bloom

I stagger along on four legs,
skeletal skewers of hiking poles
clacking amid the rocks, like

some half-formed insect with
more eyes than I ever wanted

Our climb began near dawn
after two days gathering huckleberries & paddling
past a family of mergansers looking

like they just got out of bed
without combing their hair
as we allowed clock-time to fade away

One should always climb a mountain
at its pace rather than that of the city

After climbing 5000 feet, we will stand
breathless, wide-eyed, on the expanse
of Sperry Glacier or rather

what's left of it as the glaciers
of Glacier are receding like the light
in the eyes of every mountain goat we pass

the century-old chalet where we slept
will be consumed by wildfire
just weeks later, the glaciers

will be completely gone in 15 years
& we'll have to rename this place

We-Could-Have-Acted National Park

Driving 212 *(Tympanuchus cupido)*

Out here on these South Dakota two-lanes
where the prairie chickens outnumber
the cars ten to one

& you can squint the endless
bales of hay
into ghost-herds of bison

where the horizon is a full circle
enclosing you like a
cello sonata in E minor

if you stop your truck &
take a few steps
into the sagebrush & needlegrass

you'll be swallowed by a silence
that exists nowhere else
in the world

If you stand there long enough
with the sun teaching
your shadow to dance

the grains of sand will replace
each cell of your body
one note at a time

& you will begin to understand
something
about this land

Snowbound *(Aechmophorus occidentalis)*

Looking cartoonish except
for an awareness of coming death
behind sunset-orange eyes

the Western Grebe
can only take off
from water &

a winter storm last night
brought them down
into Laurie and Billy's pasture, so

a neighbor loaded all he could find
into his truck
drove until he found open water

& placed the birds
one by one
into the hand-numbing flow

then watched them fly away
shedding droplets of almost ice
like tears

& for the first time in years
he hears his dead wife's voice:
Time for breakfast, Carl

Thompson Pass *(Meleagris gallopavo)*

Let's begin the day
listening to Brahms
in a Missoula hotel room then

the drive along the spring roiling
of the Flathead River
with tongues of fog

lolling up from mouths
of fir trees tasting the sky
Let's stop at a bar in Thompson

Falls for a pint & to find
out if the pass is open –
snow & rain & a Wild Turkey

at the roadside like a hitchhiker
but drivable if we take it slow –
& the confusion of west-

flowing rivers in place of
my habitual eastbound ones
Yesterday, a coyote

on the median testing
the limits of mortality &
the physics of steel. Tomorrow

a dark corner bar in Spokane
with bad music & too many TVs
But today, as soaring as

the Brahms as delicate as the
fog, to be here with the woman
I love with bellies full

of sushi & the lights of Coeur
d'Alene seeping through the blinds
& painting our bodies in joy

Meanwhile *(Pelecanus erythrorhynchos)*

Lifting like a fog
from the face of the river
wings torment the air

as a single line of pronghorn
lope into the shadow
of Cinnamon Mountain

the pelicans paint themselves
across the marbled sky yet somehow
        somewhere
we are still bombing children

Brackett Creek *(Aquila chrysaetos)*

Gold coins of aspen shimmer on hillsides
as a Golden Eagle lifts from a fence post

follows the slope of the land like notes
undulating across a sheet of music

Some adagio written late in the composer's life
returning to a major key for the first time in years

Sunlight painting spruces, barns & the ribboning road
unrolling before us like our best possible future

surrounded by the only gold that isn't fool's gold
we drive into the promise of love

Autumn *(Grus canadensis)*

Two days of rain
then
a pasture blanketed
with Sandhill Cranes

the world cast
in coppers & ochre
the sky broiling
with the last of the sun

A bad 70s song
comes on the radio
takes me back
to a piece of childhood

when life was
unburdened
by the memories
of itself

The cranes will soon
head south &
it would be so easy
to cry right now

much easier than
changing the station
or just
turning the damn thing off

Sandhill Crane

Today's Business *(Actitis macularius)*

Inbox:
1.   Watching each wave
        bleed through all the faces of blue
        from cobalt to teal to
        almost-fir-tree green
        until shattering white
        against the shore

2.   Watching layer upon layer
        of mountain fading
        to the ghost of a horizon,
        echoes, with only the nearest
        discernible as tree-laden

3.   Watching that single cloud
        small as a sparrow's heart
        shift & drift
        into a memory,
        lost fable of rain

4.   Watching this lone sandpiper
        working his stretch of beach
        each pebble holding a mystery
        like a scar holds a moment of bliss,
        eventually

Outbox:
1.   This pen
2.   This paper

100 Highways *(Larus occidentalis)*

Mornings on the balcony overlooking
Monterey Bay with a paper cup
of bad hotel coffee & the shrieks

of gulls from the rooftops
telling the world to wake up
before this moment is gone

forever & the cypress trees
lining the park twisted
into dervish shapes dancing

wild but at a pace of decades
between each beat
sounded by the sea

It's always this music that calls &
it only took me a hundred highways
(this time) to get here

Railroad Doves *(Columba livia ferroviae)*

One could do worse than spend the day
watching them: not quite rock
doves & not quite pigeons, evolving
along the tracks feeding
with each passing grain train
amber in prairie sunlight

The grain is long since gone &
it may be some genetic memory
keeps them clustering on these piles
of deathstone filling
the long line of the coal train
cutting our town in half

The wheeze of airbrakes powering
slap of wings like an eight of
spades in the spokes of a bicycle
& the squealing departure begins
casting off the birds & taking the poison
dust to the next town

The wind brings the stench of coal
I take it into my lungs, knock a few seconds
off the end of my life, breathe out
& in again … out & in again
The Railroad Doves gather & swirl
to a nearby rooftop, await the next train

Late tonight a dragon will swallow
the moon heedless
of the greed that swallows the world
one train at a time &
one could do worse
than to watch the doves

Railroad Dove

Domestic Feral *(Columba livia)*

Her trident feet know the pavement like
I know these four walls. We both
feed at the mercy of others, pace

like prisoners or pendulums, see
our reflections in glass buildings &
dream of cliffs. There was a time

when she was not a pigeon & I
was not a citizen, a sapiens, a wearer
of shoes & hats, & then

in the searing silence of the Badlands
I see them darting in & out of shadows
primordial, pre- & post-historic:

Rock Doves
in & of themselves, free &
fearless & I for a moment

can imagine myself barefoot
to the earth, bareheaded to the sky
unthinking fearless & free

Poem for Yusuf Eradam *(Streptopelia decaocto)*

Birds are the fish of the air, you said
the last time I drove you
back to that red house squatting
at the edge of a field strewn
with remnants of the harvest

Both of us now years older, you
back in Ankara, me across the country
to Montana where daily visits
of a Eurasian Collared Dove bring you to mind
with his call of *Allahu akbar Allahu*

akbar Allahu akbar – God is great
even though our religion is poetry
simply & nothing more
one can't help being moved
by most any kind of prayer

Today you write, *I have fed all the stray cats*
& also the dog that scares them
Yelled at the lorry driver
who cut down a tree for the parking space. But
these are mundane acts taken for granted

Allahu akbar Allahu akbar Allahu akbar

But maybe you said it was fish
who are the birds of the sea?
Either way it's good to know that you & I
under the same canopy of birdsong are still
struggling to swim this ink & paper sky

The Hands of My Father *(Dryocopus pileatus)*

This coffee won't stay hot
for long
on a morning that tastes of Autumn
at a picnic table painted
with a faint memory of blue

Through the fir trees bearded
with Spanish moss
the light from Lake Mary Ronan
weaves like a fox tracking its prey
led by the purity of hunger

An eruption of jack-hammering
& a taunting laughter
announce the arrival
of a Pileated Woodpecker
from the depth of the forest

& I'm taken back to the last time
I saw one of these
elusive hallucinatory birds
back when I was still so young
that I thought I'd live forever

that there'd be plenty of time for decisions
until one day of cold coffee & lakelight
I look down at my hands
& realize they have become
the hands of my father

Great Horned Owl

Elegy *(Bubo virginianus)*

The owls have held nightly
a dialogue across the valley

one near the house where I stand
in crackling leaves & moonlight

the other down closer
to the tongue of the river

discussing the logistics of
rabbit, the taste of flight

until

hiking today up to Deep Creek
I found one of them, broken

eyeless from ravens &
that night as expected

the conversation had ended
but in dreams, maybe

I listen to a lone owl talking
to anyone who will listen

Strangers *(Selasphorus rufus)*

Sudden buzzing & flash
of red – gone before
I have a chance to breathe

Hummingbird startles
stops my pen
the way a ringing phone

can terrify & seize –
an ice-cold hand
plunged heart-deep like a stone

sinking to the bottom
of a willow-fringed pond
where we've waited for days

to see our reflection
finding nothing but strangers
where our faces should be

Rufous Hummingbird

"No Comment" *(Melanerpes uropygialis)*

> *Never let a few facts*
> *get in the way of a good story.*
> – Ed Abbey (as quoted by Doug Peacock)

Somewhere south of Salt Lake
& north of Jalisco
east of the Hollywood sign
& west of this Gila Woodpecker
digging a new home in the arm of a cactus,
Doug & I sit at Abbey's grave
passing a warm can of cerveza
between the three of us

The bird doesn't mind the intrusion
visitations here are rare &
sometimes among the gifts
of shells & stones & hand-carved effigies
something is left that's
of use in lining a nest

I've brought a heart-shaped stone
to which I've tied a small black feather
The woodpecker eyes the string
as we finish our beer
& say our goodbyes

At this point the ornithologists
are rising in protest
because Gila Woodpeckers don't line their nest
with string or anything else
so the entire conceit of this poem
falls apart, to which I say,
quoting the words carved
into the rock marking his grave,

"No Comment"

25 Bears *(Empidonax occidentalis)*

The promise of flycatchers
hidden in the deep wood
tease of song from the shadows

The diamond light of water
breaking into river's breath
against the faces of rock

The caress of cedared wind
& undulations of fir trees
standing-room-only on a west-facing slope

The scant clouds pawing their way
across the sky-blue sky
that is nothing but sky-blue

The taste of this coffee
on the cabin's deck high above
the voicings of the Yaak River

& all the rest of it
made richer by the fact of those
remaining 25 grizzlies

somewhere
out there living
their perfect ursine lives

Without them, colors fade to sepia
sounds to a distant tin & we lose
some part of ourselves impossible

to describe to future generations
who will grow old believing
that the natural shape of their soul

is to have a cold dark nothing
lodged at its center – a hole the size
of a bear track in the spring mud

Writing at Grizfork Studio *(Pica hudsonia)*

Each day begins
with the conversations of magpies
who never run out of things to talk about

Each morning unfolds
with the fact of those mountains
who never feel the need to say a thing

I sit at my desk
with both & try to grab hold
of what lies between the two

On a good day
I come close

Black-billed Magpie

Kestrel *(Falco sparverius)*

In that moment just before
something dies

a triple rainbow is held
by the fingertips of mountains
dissolves into two, then one

a car stalls on a gravel road
and the driver sits unmoving
staring into the distant gray morning

a flock of autumn blackbirds
settles into the barren willow
that still feels the strain of where the rope once hung

the mountains release their grip
as if a child letting the string of a balloon
slide from her hand

a man at his window thinks about
the same woman as always
whenever the light is like this

and the breaking sun flashes
off the back of a hovering falcon
as it decides which troubled life to set free

Mexican, Unknown *(Aphelocoma wollweberi)*

Overgrown two-track bloodhounds its nose
up into the Chiricahua Mountains of Arizona
cresting near the gate of a forgotten cemetery
where Mexican Jays flash blue & gray
from alligator juniper to Apache pine
& many graves, unnamed, marked only
with a metal plate, letters hammer-stamped
one at a time into the rust:
"MEXICAN CHILD" or
"MINE ACCIDENT"
But the one that silences the jays,
& drifts under my fingers
like river stones:
"MEXICAN, UNKNOWN"

At the Geronimo Memorial, an obelisk
of cobblestones, a beehive that's lost
its sting, a roadside non-attraction that
doesn't mark the spot but implies
the proximity of the hero's surrender
to the America-first wall-builders of their day,
beneath the assault of Border Patrol helicopters
in a desert where they dump water tanks
to guarantee that children will die,
some beautiful Unknown has spray-painted
the three-word prayer:
Chinga la Migra
in a language of lullaby & resistance
& true as the flights of corvids

Hotel Window: Belgrade, Montana
(Corvus brachyrhynchos)

The gray view of a junkyard
spread along the black
slash of the interstate
school buses & farm implements
mostly

Coyote-brown weeds
resist the lull of snow
the welcome respite
& fenceposts fail
at their civic uprightedness

In the still dark – almost full moon
peeling away a skin of cloud –
I dropped you at the airport
returned to our room to see
if any undreamt dreams were waiting

None were &
the bed had grown cold

Like this coffee

In a ghost tree across the road
a dark shape flaps
from branch to branch then
to the ground behind
a low stone wall

It's hard not to think about death
in February

American Crow

Spinning *(Corvus corax)*

Raven holds tight to a single point of sky
& spins
longing for the dizziness of youth as when

pushed by your sister on a rainbow-painted gate
revolving
on an iron post the world whirling into something

close to nothingness. The poem unwrites
itself
as our best ones must. Haze of swallows

below the bridge & river swollen with the fetus
of spring
For a moment raven holds still as the wide sky

spins taking the earth with it. Memories are
cast off
as when you lose your grip & go tumbling

terrified & laughing across the grass of
the park
spinning into a map of a solitary point

Old Chico, Morning *(Poecile gambeli)*

Cup of coffee on the cabin's porch
between the sigh of the creek &
the hiss of aspens when

a sudden visitation of chickadees
crackles like sparks in a nearby sapling
Another drink of coffee &

scudding clouds remind me
of the sailboat I wish I hadn't sold
Another drink & narcotic sun rising

from the gulch where fools died
for gold & might again   Drink
of coffee   I was going to restore

the old boat & live half the year
island-hopping writing poems in the galley
& learning to fish

Coffee & the popcorning of slow
tires on gravel sends the birds
into someone else's poem

Phases of the Moon During the Pine Creek Fire
(Sialia currucoides)

Fire Moon #1
A moon full of water
blood-red over blackened ridge
The bar empties to watch the burning

Fire Moon #2
Gemstone fires blaze
on this full-moon but moonless night
like stars scattered across the mountain

Fire Moon #3
Bluebird on the fencepost
is bluer with this ash-haze background
while the moon sleeps

Fire Moon #4
Tattered cottonball
the moon tonight, cloud-hidden
& weary of bearing witness

Fire Moon #5
Parenthesis moon
waiting for its other half
dream-lost in the smoke

Fire Moon #6
Lost track of the moon
for a week – smoke clearing, now
it holds the last of the fire

Fire Moon #7
Ghost moon in daylight
through a Halloween landscape
Black sticks of trees still smoldering

Fire Moon #8, one year later
Crimson torches of fireweed
leaping from the greening slopes
as a new moon approaches

Dance Hall *(Poecile rufescens)*

Our rented cabin, a long-ago dance hall
so for a while I try to hear
the tapping of boots still fresh

with the reek & dust of a week's worth
of work running cattle or guiding the
transmutation of tree into lumber. Boots

stomping these floorboards in time with
fiddle & bass & piano – the
spiraling conflagration of so many

anonymous lives calling out, "I am here!"
but they're all long-buried & the plastic
flowers faded into pastels & everything

is quiet enough now to hear the song
of the Chestnut-backed Chickadee
singing from the spruce across the road

March 12, Paradise Valley *(Turdus migratorius)*

The ax finds its way
every time
through the flesh of each log

The halves open & lie down
on either side
of the chopping block

The sound of my chopping
doesn't disturb
the deer browsing in the last of the daylight

The year's first robin
visits briefly
disappears into shadows of the willow

The first beer of the evening
fits the curve
of my glove just as well as the ax

After the Storm *(Sturnella neglecta)*

Tinder bundles of cloud set ablaze
by last flare of the setting sun

Tall grasses still lost
in their dervish dance

Meadowlarks, note by note,
returning to their evening song

& my face & shoulders wet
from being too alive to go indoors

Western Meadowlark

Birds of Mexico and Central America

"If the bird is invisible,
we see the color of its song."

—Octavio Paz, "In Uxmul"

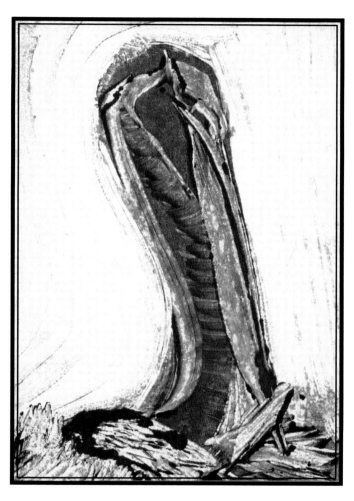

Brown Pelican

Sian Ka'an: "Where the Sky is Born"
(Pelecanus occidentalis)

A string of pelicans
like a broken rosary
slipping through the
blue hands of sky

Their flight echoes
each wave's advance
& retreat
pendulums of the world's clock

The line where sea meets sky
like the torn edge of a sheet of paper
must be the precise location
that the world ends

A barrier crossed only by sun,
moon & certain birds
Perhaps also by you & me
when drunk on madness or love

Monkey River *(Nyctanassa violacea)*

Lost in the full moon eye
of the Yellow-crowned Night Heron
as we motor our way upstream

where troops of howler monkeys
seep through the canopy of cieba trees
like a tipped cup spilling bass notes

Our guide remembers a childhood
of paddling his dugout until the
brackish water gave way to fresh

filling jugs for the day's supply
a chore reserved for the youngest
the one closest to the music

of the feathered & furred
the muddied whisperings of the river
the stone gaze of the iguana

Some days he was lazy & didn't
paddle far enough so his family
drank the salty water, scowling

This heron is the great-great-grandson
of the one who watched the lazy boy
singing monkey-songs & dipping his buckets

Mise-en-Scène *(Fregata magnificens)*

The sky slashed with
scimitars of frigatebirds

The sea falling in & out
of love with the moon

A yellow tablecloth
a red can of Tecate

a courtyard of caged parakeets
& the giggling water of a tiled *pila*

(When I swam alongside the whale shark, the world's
biggest fish, I thought it would feel more momentous.
I thought something would pass between us.)

The frigatebirds glide
along invisible determinations

Tomorrow we'll drive
into the heart of the desert

Magnificent Frigatebird

Garden Emerald, Isla Taboga *(Chlorostilbon assimilis)*

Her nest a teardrop holding
to a small chain above
the patio of our casita

Three eggs inside
stones the size of faith

I'd like to become the kind of creature
that can live without disturbing
a hummingbird on its nest

but every time I get up
for another *Balboa* she bolts
into the shadow of bougainvillea

& I drink my beer
waiting for her to return

That night the power goes out
on the entire island, the chorus
of barking dogs overwhelms

& I think, *maybe we're at war*
The only light from the freighters
waiting to enter the Panamá Canal

Or are they battleships?
Have the Americans come back?

Will I try to save
her eggs? Teach her nestlings
how to fly?

Well, I'm up anyway
Guess I'll grab one more beer

La Tortolita Común *(Columbina passerina)*

This is how one should always walk
upon the forgiving earth:

with the soft clarity & nearly silent music
of the Common Ground Dove

La Paloma Aliblanca *(Zenaida asiatica)*

One is easily
tricked
into thinking the world
a perfect
place
when woken each
morning
by the calls of
the White-winged
Dove

Kingfisher

Tapestry *(Chloroceryle amazona)*

In the jungle beyond Quepos
kingfisher weaves the air
back & forth above the silence of the pond

Warp: I've never been this old before
Weft: I'll never be this young again

The bird pauses, laughing
from a branch above its reflection
as the hidden crocodile wakes

Warp. Weft.

I laugh along to be polite
but once again I've missed the joke

This Poem is a Bowl of Water *(Pteroglossus frantzii)*

I try to find the dress you like
at the last stall of the market
where the old man is dusting toy guitars

& if you say you like the full moon
I'll get that for you as well
climbing jungle trees to where
their green fingers dance in the air

& the Fiery-billed Araçari
plucks fruit – small icons of moon-ness –
tasting more of them than I ever will

The dress I find isn't the same one
& my tree-climbing days may be over
the ground holds me tighter every day

So instead, I bring you this bowl of water
that holds the moon's undulating face,
place it into your hands
& invite you to drink

Any Other Hammer *(Pyrrhura hoffmanni)*

Each morning
the guava tree
is alive with parakeets

while *Ngäbe cafeteros*
hike the steep trails
to the coffee fields

& I wake from dreams
of never having learned
to speak English or

any other human language
any other hammer
that mistakes love

for a nail needing
to be driven home

43 Students *(Caracara cheriway)*

Driving the whiskey-red desert of Baja
marking time by utility poles
leaning under the weight
of Crested Caracaras

Back in the capital
        they are protesting the murder
                of the 43 students at Iguala

Our rental 4x4 throws dust
into the eye of the sun
on the road to Lopez Mateos
where the gray whales are nursing

Back in the capital
        the banners read *Ejército Asesino,*
                ¿Dónde están los 43 estudiantes?

A whale & her calf swim
beneath our *lancha* close enough to touch
my neck sunburnt, the salt air
reminds me of cotton candy, the boardwalk

Back in the capital
        the mothers & grandmothers
                43 names like flames on their tongues

A 6-pack of Modelo in a $20 room
shared with shy lizards that keep the mosquitoes
at bay & each beer fails to take me
any   further   away

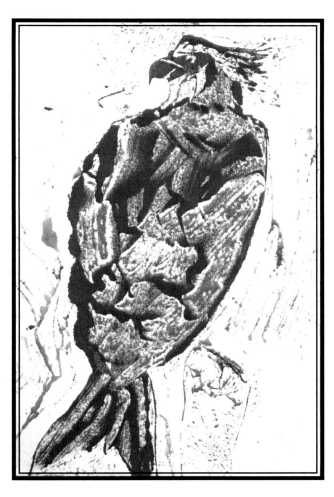

Northern Crested Caracara

New Year's Eve at the Swinging Armadillo
(Quiscalus mexicanus)

Great-tailed Grackle grips
a power line crossing overhead
The year is ending by certain clocks

By others, tonight is just another night
His bluegreenpurpleblack plumage
like the sea where the ship of days

sinks into myth, fades
into unreliable memories &
nothing can hold out against the deep

At this bar at the edge of town,
where "Hopkins Village" is shed
in favor of its old name, *Yugadan*,

a half-moon rises from the sea:
bowl of oranges & black flowers
on a tablecloth of stars

Garifuna drummers pound out
the final moments of my year
I too, have been stretched taut enough to echo

Soon winter will feel again like winter
but for now, all is music & moonlight
& the waves unfold on the dock like orchids

Birds of Europe

"In the tunnel of birdsong
a locked gate opens."

—Tomas Tranströmer, *The Sorrow Gondola*

Mute Swan

Dulce et Decorum, **Revisited** *(Cygnus olor)*

At Windsor Castle
my hand against an outer wall
wondering whose blood once stained
this particular stone?

Perhaps some ancestor of mine
a farmer pulled from his field
for some just cause no one really knew
or believed in

God was invoked – & patriotism
His crops faded, untended &
his children told the story
for a while

Later the swans gliding
across the glass of the pond
beyond the window of a pub
remain mute on the subject

Visitation *(Chroicocephalus ridibundus)*

Ankle-deep at the edge of the world
scanning the horizon for the ships
of Odysseus still seeking the homeland

The Mediterranean rolls in
one white page at a time, a mystery
of millennia, a text misunderstood

A Black-headed Gull settles
in the sand beside me, also scanning
the horizon but for his own myth

His own inscrutable purpose
has brought him to this beach
as has my own

We are both visitors
into the other's world, sharing
this *wine dark sea*, the unknowable

Shadow Wall *(Podiceps cristatus)*

The memorial stretches
along the *Nieuwe Keizersgracht*
over 200 Jewish names, or rather
Dutch names that were still
a little too Jewish

Engraved plaques set in concrete
moss-etched bricks & ants
crawling over the names
the ages & which death camp
collected their shoes, took their lives

A Great Crested Grebe
head & eyes like fire, back like ash
cuts a V through the reflections
of houses across the canal
where the murdered once lived

He dives near #12
home of Walter & Elizabeth Leib
killed at Auschwitz
first him, October 1942, then her
the following September

along with their children
Gustave, age 2 & Friede, age 1

Flying underwater
the bird catches a glimpse
of red hats & the tiki torches
of Charlottesville, gunfire at
a Walmart in El Paso

He resurfaces at #20,
home of Sara & Klara, ages 9 & 5
who were taken from this world
on a postcard-perfect day,
April 1943, at Sobibór

A Tour of the Wines of the Camargue
(Phoenicopterus roseus)

The two Mary's left the Bible
& took a boat to the south of France
landing in the place of white horses
& flamingos that hover above the marsh
like great black & red dinosaurs pinned
to the museum walls of sky

By the time I got here
they were very old & had forgotten
their native Aramaic, speaking
only French with a vague Spanish accent
They sold me a hat like the *gardiens* wear
saying it made me look a little like Van Gogh

They, of course, helped him mix his pigments
when he was here painting fishing boats
& I thought I caught sight of him
in the far stands at the bull fighting arena
but it was actually a flamingo in disguise,
in town to study the behavior of American poets

Greater Flamingo

Chant *(Columba palumbus)*

Dawn returns
to our courtyard
on her way to the sea

Darkness surrenders
not like an army
but a lover

& suddenly –
or perhaps gradually –
there is no escape

from the relentless
whoo-oo-ing
of the wood pigeon

pulling us from sleep
unready
bewildered to be alive

& for that small miracle
I am grateful
I am grateful

I am grateful

"Raft of the Medusa" *(Gallinula chloropus)*

On the way to the Louvre
walking the long formality of
the *Jardin des Tuileries*

the moorhen in the grass
poses for a photo, then
cocks an eye as if to say,

"Don't waste your time on the Mona Lisa,
mon ami, it's the Gericault
you really need to see.

"There's nothing enigmatic
about that smile," he seems to continue,
"it's just the way he painted mouths.

"You'll see for yourself
as soon as you hit the hall
beyond that circus of a room

"But trust me, *mon ami*,
the Gericault is what you crossed an ocean
to be gratefully damaged by."

Wrong Everything *(Coloeus monedula)*

The jackdaws of Amsterdam
ripple through branches
not yet in leaf
like pulses of electricity

Synapses fire – they
rouse the crow receptors
in my brain
triggering Michigan murders

First, yes, just the gathering of crows
but then unwanted memory
the other meaning
of that un-unpackable word

Two friends, Dante & Sean,
both just wrong place
wrong time wrong world
wrong guns wrong bullets

wrong belief in wrong god
wrong expectation of
wrong justice wrong
brothers in wrong graves

"Wheatfield with Crows" *(Corvus corone)*

I'd almost believe
that these canvases will tell you
what I can't say in words
–Vincent Van Gogh in a letter to Theo

Nothing prepares you
for standing before it
very nearly at closing time

It won't stop moving,
the waving wheat
the pulsating wagon tracks

& those crows
scattered letters: m, v, m, m, v
like you drew as a child

He said he was painting
extreme loneliness
this day so close to that gunshot

Walking back to our apartment
above Quellijnstraat, that crow
hopping from branch to branch

It's not loneliness
that draws me to his paintings
it's the joy, just-below

Extinct Birds

"It is very hard to give birds advice.
They are already members of eternity."

— Jim Harrison, *Returning to Earth*

Passenger Pigeon

Farm Work *(Ectopistes migratorius)*

Once an estimated 40% of all
North American birds, billion-strong flocks
of Passenger Pigeons blocking
out the sun for days

On March 24, 1900, Press Clay Southworth
a young boy on a Pike County, Ohio farm
ate his typical breakfast of
eggs and thick slabs of bacon or
a tall stack of buttermilk flapjacks maybe

Roosting in oak trees thick as leaves
large limbs would snap
come crashing to the ground
in a mind-numbing cacophony of wings

He pulled on his ordinary work boots &
slapped his customary cap on his head
The routine of his day unfolded
as it had a hundred times before
Farm life thrives on such repetition

They sold for pennies, so for much of the 18th
and 19th centuries this was the only meat
tasted by slaves & servants while masters
grew fat on hogs also fed on the flesh of the pigeons

Press made his daily rounds collecting
eggs and milking cows, slop for the pigs,
chopped wood and hauled buckets
of water from the well dug
by his father or grandfather maybe

1869, Van Buren County, Michigan:
7.5 million killed by commercial hunters
1878, Petoskey: 50,000 birds/day for five months
barrels filled boxcars shipped east

The boy noticed an unfamiliar bird
eating corn in the barnyard
grabbed his shotgun
and asked his mother's permission
He was a good shot, a natural

Pots of burning sulfur placed beneath roosting trees
fumes dazing the birds who fell to the ground for an easy
kill. With netted birds: heads crushed between thumb
and finger. It sounded like rainfall

I imagine that the farm boy noticed nothing special
about the moment he pulled the trigger
and the last one ever seen in the wild
fell to the earth holding the final word on the subject
in its half-closed scarlet eye

But it didn't matter one way or the other
the business was finished
and there was more farm work to do
and already the sun was sinking
into a slate-blue feathered horizon

CURRENT LIFE LIST/INDEX

(bold type indicates birds written about in this collection)

Ducks, Geese and Swans (*Anatidae*)
    Snow Goose (*Chen caerulescens*), 44
    Greylag Goose (*Anser anser*)
    Canada Goose (*Branta canadensis*), 6
    Mute Swan (*Cygnus olor*), 110
    Trumpeter Swan (*Cygnus buccinator*), 46
    Egyptian Goose (*Alopochen aegyptiaca*)
    Wood Duck (*Aix sponsa*)
    American Black Duck (*Anas rubripes*)
    Mallard (*Anas platyrhynchos*)
    Mottled Duck (*Anas fulvigula*)
    Blue-winged Teal (*Anas discors*)
    Cinnamon Teal (*Anas cyanoptera*)
    Northern Shoveler (*Anas clypeata*)
    Northern Pintail (*Anas acuta*)
    Redhead (*Aythya americana*)
    Common Pochard (*Aythya ferina*)
    Bufflehead (*Bucephala albeola*)
    Common Goldeneye (*Bucephala clangula*)
    Hooded Merganser (*Lophodytes cucullatus*)
    Common Merganser (*Mergus merganser*), 48
    Red-breasted Merganser (*Mergus serrator*)

Chachalacas, Curassows and Guans (*Cracidae*)
    Plain Chachalaca (*Ortalis vetula*)
    Gray-headed Chachalaca (*Ortalis cinereiceps*)

Guineafowl (*Numididae*)
    Helmeted Guineafowl (*Numida meleagris*)

New World Quail (*Odontophoridae*)
    Gambel's Quail (*Callipepla gambelii*)
    Northern Bobwhite (*Colinus virginianus*)

Partridges, Grouse, Turkeys and Old World Quail (*Phasianidae*)
    Gray Partridge (*Perdix perdix*)
    Domestic Chicken/Red Junglefowl (*Gallus gallus domesticus*)
    Ring-necked Pheasant (*Phasianus colchicus*)

Indian Peafowl (*Pavo cristatus*)
Ruffed Grouse (*Bonasa umbellus*), 47
Greater Sage-Grouse (*Centrocercus urophasianus*)
Dusky Grouse (*Dendragapus obscurus*)
Greater Prairie-Chicken (*Tympanuchus cupido*), 50
Wild Turkey (*Meleagris gallopavo*), 52

Loons (*Gaviidae*)
Common Loon (*Gavia immer*), 9

Grebes (*Podicipedidae*)
Great Crested Grebe (*Podiceps cristatus*), 112
Black-necked "Eared" Grebe (*Podiceps nigricollis*)
Western Grebe (*Aechmophorus occidentalis*), 51

Flamingos (*Phoenicopteridae*)
Greater Flamingo (*Phoenicopterus roseus*), 114

Storks (*Ciconiidae*)
Wood Stork (*Mycteria americana*)
Black Stork (*Ciconia nigra*)
White Stork (*Ciconia ciconia*)

Ibises, Spoonbills (*Threskiornithidae*)
African Sacred Ibis (*Threskiornis aethiopicus*)
American White Ibis (*Eudocimus albus*)
Glossy Ibis (*Plegadis falcinellus*)
Roseate Spoonbill (*Platalea ajaja*)

Herons, Bitterns (*Ardeidae*)
Bare-throated Tiger Heron (*Tigrisoma mexicanum*)
Black-crowned Night Heron (*Nycticorax nycticorax*)
Yellow-crowned Night Heron (*Nyctanassa violacea*), 93
Green Heron (*Butorides virescens*)
Western Cattle Egret (*Bubulcus ibis*)
Grey Heron (*Ardea cinerea*)
Great Blue Heron (*Ardea herodias*), 11
Great Egret (*Ardea alba*)
Tricolored Heron (*Egretta tricolor*)
Snowy Egret (*Egretta thula*)

Pelicans (*Pelecanidae*)
American White Pelican (*Pelecanus erythrorhynchos*), 54
Brown Pelican (*Pelecanus occidentalis*), 7, 92

Frigatebirds *(Fregatidae)*
    Magnificent Frigatebird (*Fregata magnificens*), 94

Gannets, Boobies *(Sulidae)*
    Brown Booby (*Sula leucogaster*)

Cormorants, Shags *(Phalacrocoracidae)*
    Brant's Cormorant (*Phalacrocorax penicillatus*)
    Pelagic Cormorant (*Phalacrocorax pelagicus*)
    Neotropic Cormorant (*Phalacrocorax brasilianus*)
    Double-crested Cormorant (*Phalacrocorax auritus*), 12
    European Shag (*Phalacrocorax aristotelis*)
    Great Cormorant (*Phalacrocorax carbo*)

Anhingas, Darters *(Anhingidae)*
    Anhinga (*Anhinga anhinga*), 15

New World Vultures (*Cathartidae***)**
    Turkey Vulture (*Cathartes aura*)
    Black Vulture (*Coragyps atratus*)

Ospreys (*Pandionidae***)**
    Western Osprey (*Pandion haliaetus*)

Kites, Hawks and Eagles (*Accipitridae***)**
    Egyptian Vulture (*Neophron percnopterus*)
    Swallow-Tailed Kite (*Elanoides forficatus*)
    Golden Eagle (*Aquila chrysaetos*), 55
    Sharp-shinned Hawk (*Accipiter striatus*)
    Cooper's Hawk (*Accipiter cooperii*)
    Northern Harrier (*Circus hudsonius*)
    Bald Eagle (*Haliaeetus leucocephalus*), 16
    Common Black Hawk (*Buteogallus anthracinus*)
    Mangrove Black Hawk (*Buteogallus subtilis*)
    Great Black Hawk (*Buteogallus urubitinga*)
    Roadside Hawk (*Rupornis magnirostris*)
    Broad-winged Hawk (*Buteo platypterus*)
    Swainson's Hawk (*Buteo Swainsoni*)
    Red-tailed Hawk (*Buteo jamaicensis*)
    Ferruginous Hawk (*Buteo regalis*)

Rails, Crakes and Coots (*Rallidae***)**
    Grey-necked Wood Rail (*Aramides cajaneus*)
    Common Moorhen (*Gallinula chloropus*), 117
    Eurasian Coot (*Fulica atra*)

American Coot (*Fulica americana*)

Cranes (*Gruidae*)
    Sandhill Crane (*Grus canadensis*), 56

Oystercatchers (*Haematopodidae*)
    American Oystercatcher (*Haematopus palliatus*)

Stilts, Avocets (*Recurvirostridae*)
    Black-necked Stilt (*Himantopus mexicanus*)
    American Avocet (*Recurvirostra americana*)

Plovers (*Charadriidae*)
    Semipalmated Plover (*Charadrius semipalmatus*)
    Killdeer (*Charadrius vociferus*), 13

Jacanas (*Jacanidae*)
    Northern Jaçana (*Jacana spinosa*)

Sandpipers, Snipes (*Scolopacidae*)
    American Woodcock (*Scolopax minor*)
    Whimbrel (*Numenius phaeopus*)
    Long-billed Curlew (*Numenius americanus*)
    Greater Yellowlegs (*Tringa melanoleuca*)
    Lesser Yellowlegs (*Tringa flavipes*)
    Solitary Sandpiper (*Tringa solitaria*)
    Willet (*Tringa semipalmata*)
    Spotted Sandpiper (Actitis macularius), 58
    Ruddy Turnstone (*Arenaria interpres*)
    Red Knot (*Calidris canutus*)
    Sanderling (*Calidris alba*)
    Semipalmated Sandpiper (*Calidris pusilla*)
    Western Sandpiper (*Calidris mauri*)
    Least Sandpiper (*Calidris minutilla*)
    Pectoral Sandpiper (*Calidris melanotos*)
    Dunlin (*Calidris alpina*)
    Red-necked Phalarope (*Phalaropus lobatus*)

Gulls, Terns and Skimmers (*Laridae*)
    Black Skimmer (*Rynchops niger*)
    Bonaparte's Gull (*Chroicocephalus philadelphia*)
    Black-headed Gull (*Chroicocephalus ridibundus*), 111
    Laughing Gull (*Leucophaeus atricilla*)
    Franklin's Gull (*Leucophaeus pipixcan*)
    Ring-billed Gull (*Larus delawarensis*), 19

Great Black-backed Gull (*Larus marinus*)
Western Gull (*Larus occidentalis*), 59
Yellow-footed Gull (*Larus livens*)
European Herring Gull (*Larus argentatus*)
American Herring Gull (*Larus smithsonianus*), 20
Lesser Black-backed Gull (*Larus fuscus*)
Caspian Tern (*Hydroprogne caspia*)
Royal Tern (*Thalasseus maximus*)
Common Tern (*Sterna hirundo*)
Forster's Tern (*Sterna forsteri*)
Black Tern (*Chlidonias niger*)

Pigeons, Doves (*Columbidae*)

Rock Dove (*Columba livia*), 63
"Railroad" Dove (*Columba livia ferroviae*), 60
Common Wood Pigeon (*Columba palumbus*), 116
Pale-vented Pigeon (*Patagioenas cayennensis*)
Eurasian Collared Dove (*Streptopelia decaocto*), 64
Common Ground Dove (*Columbina passerina*), 98
Ruddy Ground Dove (*Columbina talpacoti*)
White-tipped Dove (*Leptotila verreauxi*)
Mourning Dove (*Zenaida macroura*), 18
White-winged Dove (*Zenaida asiatica*), 99
Passenger Pigeon (*Ectopistes Migratorius*), 124
(stuffed specimen, under glass)

Cuckoos (*Cuculidae*)

Groove-billed Ani (*Crotophaga sulcirostris*)
Greater Roadrunner (*Geococcyx californianus*)

Owls (*Strigidae*)

Eastern Screech Owl (*Megascops asio*), 25
Great Horned Owl (*Bubo virginianus*), 22, 67
Eurasian Eagle-Owl (*Bubo bubo*)
Great Grey Owl (*Strix nebulosa*)
Burrowing Owl (*Athene cunicularia*)

Nightjars (*Caprimulgidae*)
Common Nighthawk (*Chordeiles minor*), 21

Swifts (*Apodidae*)
Chimney Swift (*Chaetura pelagica*)
White-throated Swift (*Aeronautes saxatalis*)

Hummingbirds (*Trochilidae*)
Violet Sabrewing (*Campylopterus hemileucurus*)
Lesser Violetear (*Colibri cyanotus*)
Garden Emerald (*Chlorostilbon assimilis*), 96
Stripe-tailed Hummingbird (*Eupherusa eximia*)
(Violet) Crowned Woodnymph (*Thalurania colombica*)
Rufous-tailed Hummingbird (*Amazilia tzacatl*)
Snowy-bellied Hummingbird (*Amazilia edward*)
Ruby-throated Hummingbird (*Archilochus colubris*)
Anna's Hummingbird (*Calypte anna*)
Rufous Hummingbird (*Selasphorus rufus*), 68
Scintillant Hummingbird (*Selasphorus scintilla*)
Calliope Hummingbird (*Selasphorus calliope*)

Trogons (*Trogonidae*)
Orange-bellied (Collared) Trogon (*Trogon collaris aurantiiventris*)

Kingfishers (*Alcedinidae*)
Amazon Kingfisher (*Chloroceryle amazona*), 101
Belted Kingfisher (*Megaceryle alcyon*)

Motmots (*Momotidae*)
Turquoise-browed Motmot (*Eumomota superciliosa*)

Toucans (*Ramphastidae*)
Yellow-throated Toucan (*Ramphastos ambiguus*)
Fiery-billed Araçari (*Pteroglossus frantzii*), 102

Woodpeckers (*Picidae*)
Acorn Woodpecker (*Melanerpes formicivorus*)
Golden-naped Woodpecker (*Melanerpes chrysauchen*)
Red-crowned Woodpecker (*Melanerpes rubricapillus*)
Gila Woodpecker (*Melanerpes uropygialis*), 70
Golden-fronted Woodpecker (*Melanerpes aurifrons*)
Red-bellied Woodpecker (*Melanerpes carolinus*)
Yellow-bellied Sapsucker (*Sphyrapicus varius*)
Red-naped Sapsucker (*Sphyrapicus nuchalis*)
American Three-toed Woodpecker (*Picoides dorsalis*)
Black-backed Woodpecker (*Picoides arcticus*)
Nuttall's Woodpecker (*Dryobates nuttallii*)
Downy Woodpecker (*Dryobates pubescens*)
Hairy Woodpecker (Leuconotopicus villosus)
Northern Flicker (*Colaptes auratus*), 34
Pileated Woodpecker (*Dryocopus pileatus*), 65

Caracaras, Falcons (*Falconidae*)
Northern Crested Caracara (*Caracara cheriway*), 104
American Kestrel (*Falco sparverius*), 76
Merlin (*Falco columbarius*)
Prairie Falcon (*Falco mexicanus*)
Peregrine Falcon (*Falco peregrinus*)

African and New World Parrots (*Psittacidae*)
Monk Parakeet (*Myiopsitta monachus*)
Orange-chinned Parakeet (*Brotogeris jugularis*)
Sulphur-winged Parakeet (*Pyrrhura hoffmanni*), 103
Nanday Parakeet (*Aratinga nenday*)
Scarlet Macaw (*Ara macao*)

Old World Parrots (*Psittaculidae*)
Rose-ringed Parakeet (*Psittacula krameri*)

Ovenbirds (*Furnariidae*)
Red-faced Spinetail (*Cranioleuca erythrops*)

Antbirds (*Thamnophilidae*)
Black-hooded Antshrike (*Thamnophilus bridgesi*)
Chestnut-backed Antbird (*Myrmeciza exsul*)

Tyrant Flycatchers (*Tyrannidae*)
Eastern Phoebe (*Sayornis phoebe*)
Black Phoebe (*Sayornis nigricans*)
Say's Phoebe (*Sayornis saya*)
Northern Tufted Flycatcher (*Mitrephanes phaeocercus*)
Dark Pewee (*Contopus lugubris*)
Western Wood Pewee (*Contopus sordidulus*)
Hammond's Flycatcher (*Empidonax hammondii*)
Cordilleran Flycatcher (*Empidonax occidentalis*), 72
Yellowish Flycatcher (*Empidonax flavescens*)
Great Kiskadee (*Pitangus sulphuratus*)
Boat-billed Flycatcher (*Megarynchus pitangua*)
Tropical Kingbird (*Tyrannus melancholicus*)
Western Kingbird (*Tyrannus verticalis*)
Eastern Kingbird (*Tyrannus tyrannus*)
Panamanian Flycatcher (*Myiarchus panamensis*)
Great Crested Flycatcher (*Myiarchus crinitus*)

Manakins (*Pipridae*)
Red-capped Manakin (*Ceratopipra mentalis*)

Shrikes (*Laniidae*)
Loggerhead Shrike (*Lanius ludovicianus*)
Great Grey (Northern) Shrike (*Lanius excubitor*)

Crows, Jays (*Corvidae*)
Grey Jay (*Perisoreus canadensis*)
Blue Jay (*Cyanocitta cristata*), 26
Steller's Jay (*Cyanocitta stelleri*)
Mexican Jay (*Aphelocoma wollweberi*), 77
Western Scrub Jay (*Aphelocoma californica*)
Eurasian Magpie (*Pica pica*)
Black-billed Magpie (*Pica hudsonia*), 74
Clark's Nutcracker (*Nucifraga columbiana*)
Western Jackdaw (*Coloeus monedula*), 118
Rook (*Corvus frugilegus*)
American Crow (*Corvus brachyrhynchos*), 27, 78
Fish Crow (*Corvus ossifragus*)
Carrion Crow (*Corvus corone*), 119
Northern Raven (*Corvus corax*), 28, 80
Chihuahuan Raven (*Corvus cryptoleucus*)

Waxwings (*Bombycillidae*)
Bohemian Waxwing (*Bombycilla garrulus*)
Cedar Waxwing (*Bombycilla cedrorum*)

Silky Flycatchers (*Ptiliogonatidae*)
Long-tailed Silky Flycatcher (*Ptiliogonys caudatus*)

Tits, Chickadees (*Paridae*)
Bridled Titmouse (*Baeolophus wollweberi*)
Tufted Titmouse (*Baeolophus bicolor*)
Carolina Chickadee (*Poecile carolinensis*)
Black-capped Chickadee (*Poecile atricapillus*)
Mountain Chickadee (*Poecile gambeli*), 81
Chestnut-backed Chickadee (*Poecile rufescens*), 84
Great Tit (*Parus major*)

Larks (*Alaudidae*)
Horned Lark (*Eremophila alpestris*)

Swallows, Martins (*Hirundinidae*)
Bank Swallow/Sand Martin (*Riparia riparia*)
Tree Swallow (*Tachycineta bicolor*)
Violet-green Swallow (*Tachycineta thalassina*)
Northern Rough-winged Swallow (*Stelgidopteryx serripennis*)

Barn Swallow (*Hirundo rustica*)
American Cliff Swallow (*Petrochelidon pyrrhonota*)

Goldcrests, Kinglets (*Regulidae*)
Golden-crowned Kinglet (*Regulus satrapa*)
Ruby-crowned Kinglet (*Regulus calendula*)

Wrens (*Troglodytidae*)
Rufous-naped Wren (*Campylorhynchus rufinucha*)
Cactus Wren (*Campylorhynchus brunneicapillus*)
Carolina Wren (*Thryothorus ludovicianus*)
House Wren (*Troglodytes aedon*)

Gnatcatchers (*Polioptilidae*)
Blue-grey Gnatcatcher (*Polioptila caerulea*)

Nuthatches (*Sittidae*)
Brown-headed Nuthatch (*Sitta pusilla*)
Red-breasted Nuthatch (*Sitta canadensis*)
White-breasted Nuthatch (*Sitta carolinensis*)

Treecreepers (*Certhiidae*)
Brown Creeper (*Certhia americana*)

Mockingbirds, Thrashers (*Mimidae*)
Grey Catbird (*Dumetella carolinensis*)
Northern Mockingbird (*Mimus polyglottos*)
Tropical Mockingbird (*Mimus gilvus*)
Brown Thrasher (*Toxostoma rufum*)

Starlings, Rhabdornis (*Sturnidae*)
European Starling (*Sturnus vulgaris*), 30

Thrushes (*Turdidae*)
Eastern Bluebird (*Sialia sialis*)
Western Bluebird (*Sialia mexicana*)
Mountain Bluebird (*Sialia currucoides*), 82
Townsend's Solitaire (*Myadestes townsendi*)
Black-faced Solitaire (*Myadestes melanops*)
Hermit Thrush (*Catharus guttatus*)
Wood Thrush (*Hylocichla mustelina*), 32
Common Blackbird (*Turdus merula*)
Song Thrush (*Turdus philomelos*)
Clay-colored Thrush (*Turdus grayi*)
American Robin (*Turdus migratorius*), 85

Chats, Old World Flycatchers (_Muscicapidae_)
    European Robin (_Erithacus rubecula_)

Dippers (_Cinclidae_)
    American Dipper (_Cinclus mexicanus_)

Old World Sparrows, Snowfinches (_Passeridae_)
    House Sparrow (_Passer domesticus_), 29

Finches (_Fringillidae_)
    Common Chaffinch (_Fringilla coelebs_)
    Evening Grosbeak (_Hesperiphona vespertina_)
    Grey-crowned Rosy Finch (_Leucosticte tephrocotis_)
    Purple Finch (_Haemorhous purpureus_)
    Cassin's Finch (_Haemorhous cassinii_)
    House Finch (_Haemorhous mexicanus_)
    Common Redpoll (_Acanthis flammea_)
    American Goldfinch (_Spinus tristis_)
    Lesser Goldfinch (_Spinus psaltria_)
    Pine Siskin (_Spinus pinus_)
    Yellow-crowned Euphonia (_Euphonia luteicapilla_)
    Thick-billed Euphonia (_Euphonia laniirostris_)
    Elegant Euphonia (_Euphonia elegantissima_)
    Tawny-capped Euphonia (_Euphonia anneae_)

New World Warblers (_Parulidae_)
    Ovenbird (_Seiurus aurocapilla_)
    Northern Waterthrush (_Parkesia noveboracensis_)
    Golden-winged Warbler (_Vermivora chrysoptera_)
    Flame-throated Warbler (_Oreothlypis gutturalis_)
    Tennessee Warbler (_Leiothlypis peregrina_)
    MacGillivray's Warbler (_Geothlypis tolmiei_)
    Kentucky Warbler (_Geothlypis formosa_)
    American Redstart (_Setophaga ruticilla_)
    Tropical Parula (_Setophaga pitiayumi_)
    Magnolia Warbler (_Setophaga magnolia_)
    American Yellow Warbler (_Setophaga aestiva_)
    Chestnut-sided Warbler (_Setophaga pensylvanica_)
    Yellow-rumped (Myrtle) Warbler (_Setophaga coronata_)
    Townsend's Warbler (_Setophaga townsendi_)
    Black-throated Green Warbler (_Setophaga virens_)
    Black-cheeked Warbler (_Basileuterus melanogenys_)
    Golden-crowned Warbler (_Basileuterus culicivorus_)
    Wilson's Warbler (_Cardellina pusilla_)
    Slate-throated Whitestart (_Myioborus miniatus_)

Oropendolas, Orioles and Blackbirds (*Icteridae*)

Yellow-headed Blackbird (*Xanthocephalus xanthocephalus*)
Western Meadowlark (*Sturnella neglecta*), 86
Yellow-backed Oriole (*Icterus chrysater*)
Bullock's Oriole (*Icterus bullockii*)
Baltimore Oriole (*Icterus galbula*)
Red-winged Blackbird (*Agelaius phoeniceus*), 36
Brown-headed Cowbird (*Molothrus ater*)
Melodious Blackbird (*Dives dives*)
Rusty Blackbird (*Euphagus carolinus*)
Brewer's Blackbird (*Euphagus cyanocephalus*)
Common Grackle (*Quiscalus quiscula*)
Boat-tailed Grackle (*Quiscalus major*)
Great-tailed Grackle (*Quiscalus mexicanus*), 106

Buntings, New World Sparrows and allies (*Emberizidae*)

Lark Bunting (*Calamospiza melanocorys*)
Red Fox Sparrow (*Passerella iliaca*)
Song Sparrow (*Melospiza melodia*)
Rufous-collared Sparrow (*Zonotrichia capensis*)
White-crowned Sparrow (*Zonotrichia leucophrys*)
White-throated Sparrow (*Zonotrichia albicollis*)
Dark-eyed Junco (*Junco hyemalis*), 37
Yellow-eyed Junco (*Junco phaeonotus*)
Savannah Sparrow (*Passerculus sandwichensis*)
American Tree Sparrow (*Spizelloides arborea*)
Chipping Sparrow (*Spizella passerina*)
Vesper Sparrow (*Pooecetes gramineus*)
Black-throated Sparrow (*Amphispiza bilineata*)
Green-tailed Towhee (*Pipilo chlorurus*)
Spotted Towhee (*Pipilo maculatus*)
Eastern (Rufous-sided) Towhee (*Pipilo erythrophthalmus*)
Chestnut-capped Brushfinch (*Arremon brunneinucha*)
White-naped Brushfinch (*Atlapetes albinucha*)

Tanagers and allies (*Thraupidae*)

White-lined Tanager (*Tachyphonus rufus*)
Cherrie's Tanager (*Ramphocelus costaricensis*)
Blue-grey Tanager (*Thraupis episcopus*)
Silver-throated Tanager (*Tangara icterocephala*)
Blue Dacnis (*Dacnis cayana*)
Slaty Flowerpiercer (*Diglossa plumbea*)
Yellow-bellied Seedeater (*Sporophila nigricollis*)
Yellow-faced Grassquit (*Tiaris olivaceus*)

Cardinals, Grosbeaks and allies (*Cardinalidae*)

Flame-Colored Tanager (*Piranga bidentata*)
Summer Tanager (*Piranga rubra*)
Scarlet Tanager (*Piranga olivacea*)
Western Tanager (*Piranga ludoviciana*)
White-winged Tanager (*Piranga leucoptera*)
Rose-breasted Grosbeak (*Pheucticus ludovicianus*)
Black-headed Grosbeak (*Pheucticus melanocephalus*)
Northern Cardinal (*Cardinalis cardinalis*), 38
Pyrrhuloxia (*Cardinalis sinuatus*)
Indigo Bunting (*Passerina cyanea*)
Lazuli Bunting (*Passerina amoena*)

Acknowledgments

Some of these poems were published in very different form in the chapbook *Saginaw Songs* (Ridgway Press, Detroit, 1999), *The Moon Cracks Open: A Field Guide to the Birds & Other Poems* (Heal the Earth Press, Saginaw, MI, 2008) and *Vagabond Song: Neo-Haibun from the Peregrine Journals* (Elk River Books, Livingston, MT, 2015).

For inspiration, support and undeserved kindness, I'd like to thank Rick Bass, Lisa Beaudin, Storrs Bishop, César Augusto Caballero Quiel, Billy Conway & Laurie Sargent, Yusuf Eradam, William Heyen, Allen Morris Jones, Drew Lanham, Doug & Andrea Peacock, Shann Ray, Daniel Rice, Keith Taylor and the Yaak Valley Forest Council.

I am very grateful to the editing guidance and expert suggestions of William Pitt Root, bard of the desert, and Michael Earl Craig, the greatest farrier-poet in the West.

Much of the final work on these poems was accomplished during an artist-in-residence stay in a remote Montana cabin in the shadow of Baboon Mountain, through the generosity of the Absaroka-Beartooth Wilderness Foundation (abwilderness.org).

Journals:
Avocet ("Loon Point")
The Bozone ("Railroad Doves")
Cardinal Sins ("Northern Flicker, Hwy 2," "I Declare It Spring")
CounterPunch, print edition ("Kestrel")
Cutthroat: A Journal of the Arts ("Glacier Park Toponymy" published as "Glacier Park Receding in My Rearview Mirror")

Fragile Arts Quarterly ("Another Blue," "My Bones," "Distances," "No Bird," "Linguistics")

High Desert Journal ("Progress")

Ibis Head Review ("Carbon")

Outsider ("Religion," "Writing at Grizfork Studio")

Pirene's Fountain ("What to Pray For" – Editors' Choice Award)

Shot Glass Journal ("100 Highways," "*La Tortolita Común*")

Temenos ("Messenger")

Watershed ("Farm Work")

Whiskey Island ("Mise-en-Scène") forthcoming

Whitefish Review ("Strangers," "Snowbound")

Anthologies:

Awake in the World, V.II, Riverfeet Press ("Suce Creek Symphony")

An Elk River Books Reader, Bangtail Press ("What to Pray For")

Poems Across the Big Sky, II: An Anthology of Montana Poets, Many Voices Press ("After the Storm")

Take a Stand: Art Against Hate Anthology, Raven Chronicles ("Mexican, Unknown")

Undeniable: Writers Respond to Climate Change, Alternating Current ("Carbon")

We Take Our Stand: Montana Writers Defend Public Lands, Rick Bass, editor ("Another Blue")

photo by Lisa Beaudin

Marc Beaudin is a poet, theatre artist, naturalist, bookseller, *Ulysses*-junkie, jazz-head, social anarchist and *vagabondaoist* currently living in the writer's haven of Livingston, Montana, dubbed "America's finest open-air asylum" for multiple reasons. He is the author of a hitchhiking memoir, *Vagabond Song: Neo-Haibun from the Peregrine Journals*, a poetry collection, *The Moon Cracks Open*, a novel, *A Handful of Dust*, and several poetry chapbooks and plays. Despite the available evidence, he believes the Brahms' *Violin Concerto in D* is more powerful than all the guns, smokestacks and coal trains in the world. More information, and his collection of bird photography, is available at CrowVoice.com.

Storrs Bishop is a graduate of Syracuse University, with a double major in English and art, where he concentrated on photography and printmaking — disciplines that remain at the heart of his artistic drive. Over the last 25 years, he has developed an aesthetic vision that blends digital photography with the analog processes of collage, block print, monotype, bookbinding and sometimes baling wire.

About the Monotypes

The images in this book were created on a printing press using water-based ink printed on very thin Japanese mulberry paper. To create the image the artist rolls out a thin coat of ink on a large piece of plexiglass. Using small pieces of scrap mat board, he scrapes away the ink in the areas that will show as white on the paper. That means white feathers or highlights are areas where the ink is removed and the black areas are what remains on the plexiglass. If he doesn't like how the image evolves, he rolls out a fresh layer of ink and tries again. When he likes what he sees he places the plexiglass on the press bed, sets a fresh piece of paper over it, and runs the sandwich through the press rollers to transfer the ink onto the paper.

The resulting prints are monotypes because each impression is completely unique and irreproducible. In contrast, a monoprint has reproducible printed elements, such as from a carved linoleum block, that carry through multiple copies, while other elements are changed with each imprint – colors, textures, additional papers, etc.

This process allows for a freedom of expression similar to gestural paintings and drawings. It engages a physical movement similar to dance matched with the manual dexterity of sculpting. It is messy and intricate and technically challenging. Through the manipulation of water and ink with paper and press settings, a certain chaos is controlled, or rather, negotiated, into an expression of art.

You can view the artist at work here:
www.riverfeetpress.com/monotypes

Printed in the U.S.A.

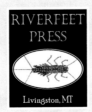

www.riverfeetpress.com